Dear Parent,

As your child encounters higher levels of reading difficulty, it is vital that he or she not only follows along with the text, but also understands the meaning of what is being read. Comprehension is often very difficult for young readers, but practice is proven to develop it. Here to help your child with reading comprehension skills are almost 100 pages of questions that accompany short stories and other passages of interest to fourth-graders.

This colorful workbook features entertaining readings followed by activities that will help your child focus on key skills such as: determining the sequence of events; differentiating between fact and opinion; and identifying the meaning of vocabulary words in context. He or she will practice a range of test-taking formats, too—from multiple-choice and sequencing to fill-in-the-blanks and completing charts.

The activities are designed for your child to handle alone, but you can read along and help with any troublesome words, ideas, or questions. Patience is key for reading comprehension. Then together you can check answers at the back of the workbook, and you should always give praise and encouragement for his or her effort. In addition, try to find other ways for your child to practice reading comprehension. You can leave a note that describes what fun activities you and your child will do first, second, and third that day. Later, have your child read a bedtime story to you, and then ask him or her some questions about it. Remember that reading is everywhere, so just use your imagination!

Mini Golf

A huge mini golf course has just opened in town. It's so big that the term *mini* cannot even describe it. All the kids are excited about the new golf course.

The course is 36 holes. That's big! Most mini golf courses are 18 holes. It took two months for the course to be built. The course has a waterfall, a dragon, and a spaceship that swallows up golf balls.

Saturday was the grand opening and no one was turned away. At the grand opening, Mega Mini Golf let the first 100 mini golfers play for free. The 100th golfer got a free Mega Mini Golf T-shirt and a free summer pass that is good any time. Once a month there will be a "Backward Day," when mini golfers will get to play the course backward.

A lot of kids and their parents were out playing on the course on opening day. That included the town's mayor! It took him 6 shots to finish hole 26 with his two sons. He said he was thrilled the golf course was finally open, even though his own game needs a little practice.

On the Fourth of July this year, there will be a Mega Mini Golf fireworks display. The golf course will be open until 1:00 AM that night only. Tickets are being sold in advance for that night. A large turnout is expected. I already bought tickets. See you there!

GRADE
4

who   what   where

when   FLASH   how

FORWARD

READING

fact   opinion

Written by **Kathy Furgang**

Illustrations by **Judy Stead**

Flash Kids™

Spark Publishing™

Spark Publishing
A Division of Barnes & Noble
120 Fifth Avenue
New York, NY 10011
www.sparknotes.com

ISBN-13: 978-1-4114-0706-0
ISBN-10: 1-4114-0706-7

For more information, please visit *www.flashkidsbooks.com*
Please submit changes or report errors to *www.flashkidsbooks.com/errors*

Printed and bound in the United States

1   3   5   7   9   10   8   6   4   2

Read each question. Circle the correct answer.

1. What is the name of the new mini golf course?

  a. New Mini Golf

  b. Spaceship Golf

  c. Mega Mini Golf

  d. The new course does not have a name.

2. Which of the following is **not** an attraction at the new golf course?

  a. waterfall

  b. dragon

  c. spaceship

  d. helicopter

3. Who was spotted playing golf at the grand opening?

  a. the president

  b. the mayor

  c. the principal

  d. a reporter

4. How many holes does the new golf course have?

  a. 18

  b. 22

  c. 32

  d. 36

5. For what event are tickets being sold in advance?

  a. grand opening

  b. Flag Day celebration

  c. Fourth of July fireworks

  d. Backward Day

6. Who received a free T-shirt at the grand opening?

  a. the first customer

  b. the 100th customer

  c. the mayor

  d. every golfer

Special Effects

Suppose you go see a movie with monsters. Or maybe you go see a movie with aliens or space battles. Are you seeing something real on the screen? Moviemakers use special effects to make things appear real on film. How do moviemakers create these amazing special effects?

Special effects in movies have been used since the early days of Hollywood. Even fake blood or makeup is a kind of special effect. Costumes are another kind of special effect. An actor in an animal suit used to scare early moviegoers who thought the animal was real!

Background paintings were another early way to make special effects. Actors could stand on a movie set with a painting of mountains behind them. The best background paintings looked just like the real thing. When we watch old movies, we often do not notice the paintings because they blend so well into the rest of the set.

More recently, moviemakers began to make models to show things that were too hard to film in real life. A small model of a town can be made. Then it can be flooded or blown up as it is being filmed. The angle of the camera makes a good model look life-size.

Today, actors can look like they are talking to characters that are made totally from special effects. The computer can make models of creatures based on real-life models. Once the movements of the creature are programmed into the computer, anything is possible. The actors pretend they are acting with the creature, but they are really acting in front of a screen. The effects are added later on a computer to make it look like the actor and the creature were together. Space battles, storms, explosions, and just about anything else can be made by computer special effects. So the next time you go to the movies, ask yourself: Was that real?

Answer the questions below.

1. What are special effects?

_____

2. What were some of the earliest special effects?

_____

3. Why do moviemakers make models?

_____

4. How do computers make special effects look real today?

_____

5. What does the word _blend_ from paragraph 3 mean?

_____

6. How do actors look like they are talking to a character made of special effects?

_____

Joe's Roadster

Joe loves cars. He has been working on his own roadster for years. A roadster is a car that is built with an open top, a single seat in the front, and a large trunk in the back. Every weekend he works on it in his garage. On nice days he pulls it out into his driveway and works under the hood. Sometimes people stop as they drive past his house and tell Joe what a beautiful car he has. This makes Joe very proud of his work.

Joe has always dreamed of entering the car in a car show. He goes to the local car show every year. This year Joe just thought he would drive his car there and park it in the parking lot.

The car show was very big this year. Many people from around the country had come to show their cars. Joe got to see hot rods, muscle cars, and even some custom-built cars similar to his own roadster.

Joe walked around and saw more cars. One car was a large van for a family. It had a built-in tent that popped up out of the roof. Another car had a built-in radio in the back that could be taken out for parties.

Joe wasn't sure that his car could win any of the prizes at the show. He felt nervous about entering the car. What if all of his hard work did not pay off? What if he did not win anything?

"Wow, great car," someone said as they walked past Joe's car in the parking lot. *Maybe I should not feel so nervous about entering the car*, he thought with a smile on his face.

Answer the questions below.

1. How does Joe feel about his roadster?

_____

2. What dream does Joe have for his car one day?

_____

3. Why do you think Joe is interested in seeing the other cars at the car show?

_____

4. How does Joe feel about entering his car in the show?

_____

5. What kinds of cars did Joe see at the show?

_____

6. How does Joe feel at the end of the story?

_____

History of Baseball

The New York Knickerbockers, founded in 1845, was the first modern baseball team. The team is believed to be the first to use the rules we know today. They set up a list of rules called the "Knickerbocker Rules." It put many of the rules that people had been using for years into written form. There was one big difference between these rules and ones that clubs before it had used. In the past, someone in the field could get a runner out by hitting them with the ball. The Knickerbocker Rules did not allow this, making the game much safer.

The first real group of baseball teams was named the National Association of Base Ball Players. By the time of the Civil War, there were nearly 100 teams from around the country in the group. Baseball helped bring soldiers together for fun at a very hard time in American history. This was the first time the game was played on a national level. Teams from different parts of the country played each other.

All the players in the National Association of Base Ball Players were amateurs. That means they were not paid for playing and only played as a hobby. In 1871, the association called the National Association of Professional Base Ball Players was founded. It was thought of as the first real major league baseball association.

Baseball has seen many changes over the years. The most important change was that it kept getting more and more fans as the years went on. Although there have been versions of the game in other countries, the game we know today as baseball is an all-American sport.

Complete each sentence.

1. The first modern baseball team was the _____.

2. Before the "Knickerbocker Rules," a player could get a runner out by

_____.

3. The National Association of Base Ball Players had about

_____ teams by the time of the Civil War.

4. During the Civil War, baseball was played by _____.

5. The National Association of Professional Base Ball Players was founded in

_____.

6. As time passed there were _____ baseball fans in
the United States.

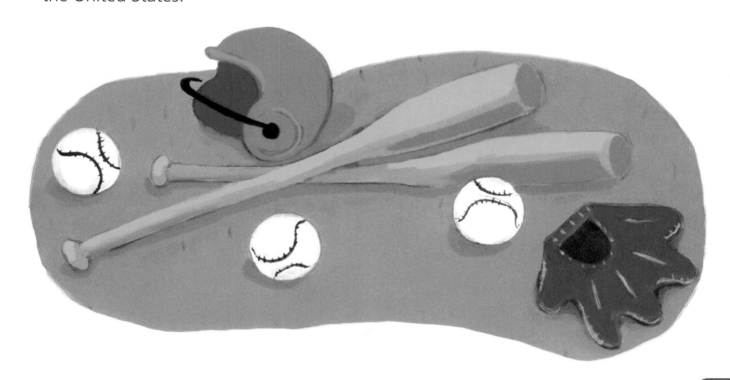

The Big Snow

Dear Grandma,

There are more than ten feet of snow on the ground here! It is even snowing right now as I write you this letter. I know it never snows where you live in Florida, but here it snows every winter. Even so, it has never snowed this much while I have been alive. Mom says it has never snowed this much since she has been alive either.

First, we got a storm two weeks ago with more than three feet of snow. That storm closed the schools for three days. When everyone dug out of that storm, it snowed again! The snow just kept falling and falling for days and days. The mayor said it had snowed three more feet. Everything was closed so we could dig out of that storm. Before we could even catch our breath, another huge storm came! It dropped two more feet of snow. The snow keeps piling up. The governor said it is now an emergency and that people will be coming here just to help us dig out all the snow.

Dad has been running the snowblower for days. He is afraid that if he lets the snow get too deep, he will not be able to get his car out of the driveway. Mom said he should not be driving in this weather anyway.

I put some snow in a bag to keep it frozen until you come here in July so you can see some snow from the biggest storm we have ever had. It has broken all the records for this state. I want to go out to build the biggest snowman ever when it stops snowing. Mom told me to tell you we will send you some pictures soon.

Love,

Emily

Answer the questions below.

1. What is the problem being written about in the letter?

_____

2. What is the author's purpose for writing the letter?

_____

3. Why doesn't Grandma's town have the same problem as Emily's?

_____

4. What does the saying *catch our breath* in paragraph 2 mean?

_____

5. Why does Emily want to save snow in a bag?

_____

6. What memories do you have of a storm where you live?

_____

Laser Tag

In what game can players shoot each other without getting hurt? Laser tag! Laser tag is a sport that has been around since the late 1970s. The United States Army first used it as a target system to train soldiers. In laser tag, you can shoot at a still target. It works because your weapon in the game shoots out a special light called an infrared light. If you aim and shoot at a target that senses this light, you made a hit! The game uses the same kind of system that lets you change TV channels with your remote control. Your gun acts as the remote. You and the other players wear targets that act like the sensors on your TV. The only real laser used is a laser for aiming at a target. The system lets players program the game in many ways and also scores the points for the players.

Kids all around the world started using laser tag in the mid-1980s. It was sold for use at home. You could play it anywhere, either inside or outside. The sport became very popular. Today there are laser tag arenas all over the country. You can go to these places with a group and play an indoor or outdoor game. Players of all ages can enjoy the sport at any time of the year.

Read each question. Circle the correct answer.

1. Who was the first to use laser tag?

   a. kids in Atlanta, Georgia

   b. toy companies

   c. the United States Army

   d. kids in Australia

2. What is the main idea of the reading?

   a. Laser tag is a dangerous sport.

   b. Laser tag is a fun and safe sport.

   c. Laser tag can be used for training soldiers.

   d. Laser tag uses a light to aim at a target.

3. What is the author's purpose for the reading?

   a. to convince people not to play laser tag

   b. to inform people about laser tag

   c. to inform people about the rules of laser tag

   d. to entertain people with stories about laser tag

4. How does the infrared light used in laser tag work?

   a. like the light in your refrigerator

   b. like the light switch in your garage

   c. like the remote control to your TV

   d. like the light that shines in your eyes

5. What kind of reading is this?

   a. nonfiction

   b. fiction

   c. poetry

   d. a play

6. When did laser tag become popular as a game that could be played at home?

   a. early 1970s

   b. late 1970s

   c. mid-1980s

   d. late 1980s

Dear Mr. Mayor

Dear Mr. Mayor,

I am writing this letter to ask you to make a new rule for Lincoln Park. I happen to be a dog lover, but I cannot stand when dogs in the park are not on leashes. I find it to be very rude when owners allow their dogs to run free through the park and bother other people.

Yesterday, a dog ran up to my son and licked him on the face. My son is allergic to dogs. His face blew up like a balloon. I had to take him home right away to give him medicine. We never even found out who the owner of the dog was.

I am not just trying to get dogs on leashes for my son. I think everyone in the park would like this rule. Dogs should not be running through baseball and soccer games at the park. It stops the game and it is also dangerous for the dog.

Lincoln Park is right on Main Street. I am sure some dogs have run out of the park and into the busy street. This is a real danger for both the dog and the people trying to drive their cars down the road.

I do not think I have to tell you what a mess the dogs make. The owners do not clean up after their dogs when they are not on a leash. This makes a mess for everyone at the park.

I am not asking for you to ban dogs from the park. I just want the dog owners to keep their pets on leashes. I think a rule like this will help the park. It should stay a good place for the whole community to gather and have a good time. Thank you.

Sincerely,

Mrs. Franklin

Write an effect to each cause on the chart.

Cause	Effect
1. Dog licks boy's face.	
2. Dogs run through baseball and soccer games.	
3. Lincoln Park is right on Main Street.	
4. Owners do not clean up after their dogs.	

Answer the questions below.

5. What is the author's purpose for writing the letter?

_____

_____

6. Write one fact and one opinion from the letter.

_____

_____

Garbage Night

Ozzie's twelfth birthday is next week. His dad told him that he could soon get a better allowance. All he had to do was some more work around the house. Ozzie thought about the work he would have to do. He would probably have to learn to do laundry and wash dishes. He wanted to tell his dad that his current allowance was just fine with him.

Then Ozzie thought about the comic books he wanted to buy. If he had a better allowance, he would be able to buy more comic books without asking his parents for money. It would be up to him to buy what he wanted. Ozzie thought about the good and bad parts of doing more around the house. He decided he should do as much as he could so he could get more allowance money.

On his first night of being twelve, Ozzie's dad told him it was garbage night. One night each week the garbage had to be put out in front of the house so that the garbage collectors could pick it up the next morning. Ozzie's dad taught him how to collect all the garbage from around the house and bring it to the curb.

Ozzie had no trouble with this new assignment. First, he went around the house and gathered the garbage bags he saw. He went from room to room. He looked in the kitchen and bathrooms. Then he tied them up and brought them to the garbage can. He tipped the garbage can back and rolled it down the driveway to the curb. *That should do it*, he thought. *This will be a great way to get my new comic books!*

Answer the questions below.

1. Why did Ozzie's dad want to give him a bigger allowance?

_____

2. What did Ozzie first think of his dad's idea?

_____

3. What made Ozzie change his mind about the extra allowance money?

_____

4. How did Ozzie buy his comic books before he got a raise in his allowance?

_____

5. When did Ozzie's dad teach him about taking out the garbage?

_____

6. What steps did Ozzie follow to put out the garbage?

_____

_____

Life on the Farm

My name is Sally and I live on a farm with my mom and dad. Life has been very hard for us. Last year we traveled all the way here from the east. It took us months just to get here. When we finally arrived my dad got to work right away building a small house and a farm. Soon we had some animals like chickens, a few mules, and a cow.

Dad used mules to plow the field. There he planted corn. In the summer he planned to harvest it and sell it to townspeople. We would use the money to buy more food and supplies.

But things did not go well at all. It did not rain for a very long time and all the corn crops failed. This made Mom and Dad very worried. Many nights while I was falling asleep I could hear them talking about what was going to happen to the farm.

Then last week Mom came and told me that we will be moving soon to a place farther to the west called California. She said the trip will be long and hard. But when we get there we will start over and build a new house. She said that Dad has sold all the animals except for the few mules. They are going to pull our wagon all the way to California. She hopes that Dad will be able to find gold! Mom said that gold is a rare metal and that a lot of it has just been found in California. Many people are moving there because of it.

I told her I was happy as long as I was with them. I guess there will be a lot more traveling ahead of us.

Write an effect to each cause on the chart.

Cause	Effect
1. Life is hard for the family.	
2. Family buys mules.	
3. There is no rain for a long time.	
4. Sally's mom and dad talk about the future of the farm.	
5. Gold is found in California.	
6. All the animals are sold except for the mules.	

Pluto

How many planets are there? You may have learned that there are nine planets in our solar system, but in August of 2006, scientists decided that Pluto did not move, or orbit, like all the other planets. Pluto is now called a dwarf planet. New things are always being found about space and our solar system. In fact, we really haven't known about Pluto for too long.

Pluto was first discovered in 1930. A scientist spotted it during a project at the Lowell Observatory in Arizona. Then other scientists around the world looked at it too. They decided that a new planet had been found.

People had plenty of ideas about what to name this dark and cold place. Names such as Zeus and Lowell were given. The three choices that were voted on were Minerva, Cronus, and Pluto. Members of the Lowell Observatory all voted. Pluto got every vote. An 11-year-old girl from England gave the winning name. She got a prize of about 10 dollars for coming up with it.

Pluto was the farthest and smallest of the planets. Pluto is made mostly of rock and ice. It was first thought that Pluto had only one moon. But in 2005, two more moons were found.

Little is known about Pluto because it is so far from Earth that it is hard to explore. It is so far away astronauts cannot be sent. A robotic spacecraft called New Horizons is on its way to Pluto. It is expected to fly by Pluto in the year 2015. What can you imagine that we will find out about this far-reaching part of our solar system?

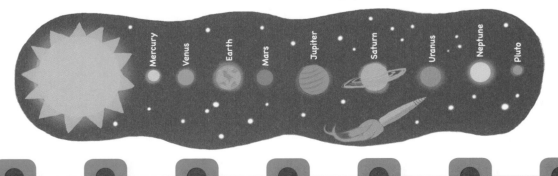

Read each question. Circle the correct answer.

1. When was Pluto discovered?

   a. 1930

   b. 2005

   c. 2006

   d. The date is unknown.

2. Who thought of the name Pluto?

   a. a scientist from Arizona

   b. scientists from around the world

   c. an 11-year-old girl from England

   d. a woman named Minerva

3. Why is Pluto no longer a planet?

   a. It is too far from the Sun.

   b. It is too far from Earth.

   c. It no longer moves.

   d. It moves differently from the other planets.

4. Which was **not** a choice for the name of Pluto?

   a. Arizona

   b. Minerva

   c. Zeus

   d. Cronus

5. What is Pluto made up of?

   a. rock

   b. ice

   c. rock and ice

   d. water and rock

6. How will Pluto be explored in the year 2015?

   a. Scientists will observe it through a telescope.

   b. A spacecraft will fly by there.

   c. Astronauts will be sent there.

   d. Pluto will not be explored at all.

Outdoor Movie Night

Friday was outdoor movie night and Julia could not wait. Julia's dad had borrowed a projector from work. He was allowing Julia to have a few friends over to watch a film on the side of the house after it got dark. Julia had invited her best friends Stacey, Carrie, Cindy, and Liz. She also invited a few boys. So far, Cindy and Bill had both called to say they would not be able to make it. Cindy was going away for the weekend with her family. Bill had guests coming over from Spain.

Julia would let her friends pick the film they wanted to watch when they got there on Friday. For now she was just thinking about everything she needed to get for the party. Her mom said that getting ready for a party was important for welcoming your guests.

Julia and her mom made a list. Cups, plates, chips, drinks, cookies, and popcorn were the first things they thought of. Then they added chairs and insect spray to the list. They also needed a big white bedsheet to show the movie against. Julia wrote everything down.

Then Julia and her mom went shopping to pick up everything on the list. They found what they needed all in one store. Julia's mom even found some big plastic bowls. They were not on the list, but they would come in handy for the snacks. They even had big lids to cover them so bugs would not get in.

Finally it was Friday. Julia's friends began to arrive as the sun was setting. They voted on a movie and the winner was *The Wizard of Oz*. Julia was glad that all of her preparations had paid off. Her dad started up the film. Movie night had begun!

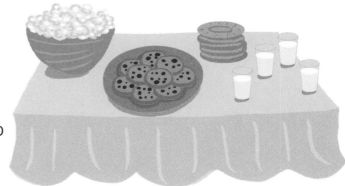

Answer the questions below.

1. Why did Julia's mom think it was important to get ready for a party?

_____

2. What were Julia and her friends going to do at the party?

_____

3. What kind of food would Julia be serving to her guests?

_____

4. What did the guests vote about, and what was decided?

_____

5. What did Julia and her mom buy that was not on their shopping list?

_____

6. How did Julia feel when Friday finally came?

_____

Pizza

Pizza was invented in Italy, right? Actually, the Greeks were really the first to eat this flat, round bread. They topped the bread with herbs, spices, and oil. Then they baked it.

This cheap and filling meal was popular in Greece. It then made its way to Italy in the 1700s. There it became known as pizza. The breads were sold on the street to the poor. The food could be picked up and eaten easily and neatly with the hands.

In the late 1800s, Italy's Queen Margherita toured Italy to observe the kingdom. She saw people eating these flat breads on the streets. So she tasted one herself. She enjoyed it so much that she asked a chef named Raffaelle Esposito to make a pizza for her to enjoy in her palace.

The chef was honored to do this favor for the queen. He decided to make the queen a special pizza. He topped the queen's pizza with fresh tomato, mozzarella cheese, and basil leaves. He chose these foods especially for their color. Red, white, and green are the colors of the Italian flag. His creation was the first modern pizza. Esposito's pizza became popular throughout Italy because people heard that it was the queen's favorite food.

So how did this tasty bread make its way to the United States? The dish did not become popular in this country until after World War II. American soldiers in Italy had tasted the food and loved it. They returned home wanting a taste of this delicious food in their own country. That's how the Italian pizzeria became a popular American tradition.

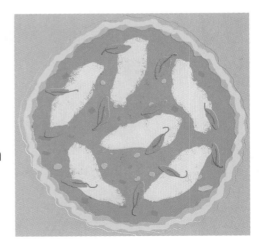

Number the events in the correct order according to the reading.

_____ Raffaelle Esposito made a special pizza for the queen.

_____ Queen Margherita tasted a pizza for the first time.

_____ American soldiers tasted pizza in Italy.

_____ The Greeks enjoyed flat, baked breads.

_____ Pizza became a popular food in the United States.

_____ Pizza became a popular meal sold in Italy's streets.

Alex the Giraffe

Alex was a giraffe who lived in a zoo with his mom, dad, and other giraffe friends. As Alex grew he noticed the necks of the other giraffes. His neck was the shortest by far! He began to get worried. His mother told him that he was unique and special. She said it did not matter how short or long his neck was.

Alex tried not to think about his short neck. But as his friends grew taller and taller, his neck stayed short. Sometimes the other giraffes teased him. His parents told him not to worry. They said that he should be happy with himself the way he is. He tried, but he could not even play in some giraffe sports. He was just too short.

One day one of the zoo workers came and took Alex away. Alex was frightened. Would he have to leave the zoo because he was not a normal giraffe? The zoo worker calmed Alex down and gave him some food. He felt better. Then he led Alex into another area of the zoo. Soon Alex's parents came to see him.

"I told you that you were special," his mother said. "The zoo has made a place just for you because so many people want to see how special you are!" She was right. Zoo visitors pointed to him and smiled and waved. They looked happy to see something so unique and special at the zoo.

Alex was allowed to go back and forth and see his friends whenever he wanted. There was a small door between the two areas. The long-necked giraffes were on one side of the door, and the short-necked giraffe was on the other. And guess who was the only giraffe that could fit through the door?

Circle the word that **best** describes the characters in the reading.

1. Alex at the beginning of the reading

happy   worried

2. Alex's parents

angry   helpful

3. Alex's friends

carefree   worried

4. Alex when he was first brought to his new area

scared   excited

5. The zoo worker

caring   mean

6. Alex at the end of the reading

happy   worried

The Cave of Lascaux

One September day in 1940, four teenage boys were hiking in the woods in southern France. They walked up to the top of Lascaux Hill and came upon a hole in the ground where a tree had fallen. They moved some of the earth around the hole. To their surprise, they found an underground cave. They uncovered the cave and walked in. There they discovered something that would surprise the whole world.

Inside the cave were paintings on the rock walls. Most of the paintings were of animals such as bulls, horses, cats, birds, and bears. The large cave was made of room after room, each with a different kind of animal painted on it.

Scientists came to the scene to study the walls. People made the paintings in 15,000 or 13,000 B.C.E. The caves were likely the only homes these people had. They may have painted on the walls to tell stories. They may have decorated the walls to look good. Were the paintings art or a way to communicate? Scientists still wonder about this question today.

The cave was opened for the public to visit. But 1,200 visitors a day had an effect on the paintings. The gas people breathe out of their bodies, called carbon dioxide, began to damage the paintings. The cave had to be closed to the public in 1963. In 1983, a copy of the cave was made so that people could once again explore this ancient world.

There are other cave paintings from this time period. Scientists can compare these caves with others like them. This is how we learn about the lives of the people who lived long ago.

Write an effect to each cause on the chart.

Cause	Effect
1. Boys go hiking in the woods.	
2. Scientists study the cave paintings.	
3. Cave opens to the public.	
4. People breathe out carbon dioxide in the cave.	
5. Cave is closed to the public.	
6. Scientists compare different cave paintings from around the world.	

Zack, the New Kid

I'm Zack. I am the new kid at school. Since kindergarten, I have been the new kid at school five times. It seems like every time I go to a new school I feel the same way. First, I worry that I won't make new friends. Next, I get to the school and I worry that I won't like my teacher or my class. After that, I worry that my teacher won't like me.

Well, this time I am taking a new attitude. I don't care who likes me. I don't care what the school is like. And I don't care what any of the kids are like. It seems that everyone is the same no matter where you go. There are some nice kids and some mean kids. There are funny kids and smart kids. I can get along with any of them. Some kids love when there's a new kid in class. Other kids hate it. I always find the kids who like that something new is happening and I hang out with them.

I'm not into sports because all the kids on the teams have known each other their whole lives. And I never stay long enough to become a good player. This may all sound sad or weird to you, but that's just the way things go. One day all of these kids will have to go to a new school and they could have a really tough time. I got used to it all when I was really young. Now I can go to school and just try to get good grades. I always make good friends, too. I don't make friends with huge groups of kids. There's always someone who wants to be my friend. That's all I need!

Read each statement. Write *true* or *false*.

1. Zack has been to five new schools since kindergarten. _____

2. Zack thinks kids are mostly the same no matter where you go. _____

3. Zack is trying to have a new attitude about being the new kid. _____

4. Zack loves sports. _____

5. Zack does not make friends easily. _____

6. Zack would just like to think about getting good grades at school. _____

Take Your Vitamins

You've heard it before: "Take your vitamins! They keep you healthy and strong!" But what vitamins do our bodies need? What do they do, and where can we get them?

Vitamin C keeps you from getting a cold. You can find it in fruits such as oranges, strawberries, and mango. It's also in vegetables such as spinach, broccoli, and snow peas.

Vitamin D is good for your bones. It is found in eggs, milk, and some fish. You can even get it from sunlight. Vitamin A helps your eyesight, skin, and teeth. Try some carrots, tomatoes, sweet potatoes, or pumpkins for this vitamin.

The vitamin folate is important in making new cells in your body. You can find that in green beans, broccoli, spinach, and several other kinds of beans.

There are about eight different kinds of B vitamins, and they all help give your body energy. Spinach has seven of them. Also try lean beef, chicken, or tuna. Eggs, milk, sunflower seeds, and soymilk are also good sources of B vitamins.

Vitamin E keeps your body's cells healthy. Plant oils, avocados, and whole grains are what you're looking for here.

With all of these different vitamins in foods, it's no wonder a variety of foods is a good idea. Many foods have several vitamins and keep your body healthy in many ways. The key to a healthy diet is to eat healthful foods. Your body will do the rest on its own.

Complete the chart with information from the reading.

Vitamin	How it helps the body	Found in
Vitamin A		
Vitamin B		
Vitamin C		
Vitamin D		
Vitamin E		
Folate		

The Passport Photo

Erica and her family were going on vacation. They would be going to France, Italy, England, and Spain.

"Let's go get your passport," said Mom. "You won't get out of the airport without one." Mom told Erica that a passport is a document with your picture on it. "You have to show it every time you come and go from the country. Each time you arrive at a new country, you get a stamp with the name of the country on it."

Erica was excited. The passport would make her feel like a world traveler. She began to think about what her passport picture might look like.

She looked through her closet for the best outfit to wear for the picture. "It's just a picture from your neck up," said Mom. "We don't have time to pick out clothes. You won't even be able to see them in the photo."

Erica ran to the bathroom mirror. She combed her hair. She put on lip gloss. *Should I wear my hair up or down?* she thought. *What about a hat?* She raced to her room.

"Erica, we're late!" Mom yelled from the front door. Erica could hear Mom's car keys dangling together.

Okay, there's no time for a hat, Erica thought. She raced out the door and they were in the car and on their way in no time.

"This passport photo will last for 5 years," said Mom. "You won't need another one until you are 17 years old."

"What!" screamed Erica. "My hair looks terrible today! I can't take my world traveler photo today. It will make me look bad for 5 years!"

Mom laughed. "Don't be so vain, little lady. It's just a passport picture. It won't be framed for everyone to see."

"I guess you're right," said Erica. "But in 5 years I'll make sure I'm ready for my picture."

Read each question. Circle the correct answer.

1. Mom describes Erica as *vain* in paragraph 10. What is the meaning of this word?

a. concerned with traveling

b. concerned with looks

c. happy

d. sad

2. Which shows the **best** example of why Erica is vain?

a. She wants to go on vacation.

b. She is late.

c. She is excited to be a world traveler.

d. She worries a lot about how her hair looks.

3. Why does Erica need a passport?

a. She is going to the mall.

b. She is getting her hair done.

c. She is going out of the country.

d. She is getting her photo taken.

4. How many stamps will Erica have on her passport when she returns from vacation?

a. 1

b. 2

c. 3

d. 4

5. What did Erica want to wear in her passport photo?

a. earrings

b. a necklace

c. a hat

d. a scarf

6. Which is **not** a country where Erica's family will go on their vacation?

a. Canada

b. Italy

c. France

d. England

E-mail Shortcuts

You get an e-mail from a friend. You would love to chat, but your fingers cannot type as fast as your mouth can talk. Do you wish there was a shortcut to help you say everything you want to say quickly? There is!

Here is a list of e-mail phrases and their shortcuts. They are very widely used. The person you are writing to just needs to know about them also! In some ways, it's like an e-mail secret code!

Abbreviation	Meaning
AFAIK	As far as I know
BFF	Best friends forever
BFN	Bye for now
CYE	Check your e-mail
EOD	End of discussion
FOFL	Fall on the floor laughing
G2G	Got to go
GR8	Great
HOAS	Hold on a second
IAC	In any case
IMO	In my opinion
JC	Just curious
JK	Just kidding

Abbreviation	Meaning
LOL	Laugh out loud
MYOB	Mind your own business
OMG	Oh my gosh
OTOH	On the other hand
POS	Parent over shoulder
QT	Cutie
TBC	To be continued
TC	Take care
W/E	Whatever
WTG	Way to go
XOXO	Hugs and kisses
YW	You're welcome
ZZZ	Sleeping

Rewrite the sentences.

1. The baby is a real QT. But AFAIK, right now she is ZZZ.

_____

_____

2. You and I are BFF. And IMO, you should CYE every day to see if I've written.

_____

_____

3. IAC, I was JK about telling you to MYOB. You are a GR8 friend and always make me LOL.

_____

_____

4. OMG, that was the funniest movie. We were all FOFL. WTG for choosing it for us.

_____

_____

5. HOAS, my mom is calling. I've G2G; it's time for dinner.

_____

_____

6. Sorry, this is the EOD. XOXO, and BFN.

_____

_____

The Beaver Water Park

One day a beaver named Chuck thought up the idea of a water park made by beavers and for beavers. All the beavers loved the idea and they got to work right away. They started by damming up a nearby river and creating a huge lake. It took years to complete but it was worth it. They named it the Log River Water Park. It was the first of its kind. The water park was hidden from people and it ran all year long. It was powered by water that was backed up from the big beaver dam.

The Bouncing Beaver family left home one morning to head to the water park. They locked up their small home. They traveled many miles through forests and across roads. It took them two days but finally they arrived at the Log River Water Park.

The Bouncing Beaver family could not believe their eyes when they got there. It was the most amazing thing they had ever seen. There were dozens of water slides all made out of wood cut by beavers. The slides twisted and looped and turned and ended at the stream far below the huge dam. There were also many small pools, underwater tunnels, and even fountains. It took them all day to explore everything.

At the end of the day they stayed in small beaver cabins on the opposite side of the lake. They stayed for two days and went home. They all agreed it was the best vacation they had ever taken.

Answer the questions below.

1. Where did the Bouncing Beaver family go for vacation?

_____

2. Who thought of the idea for the park?

_____

3. Who made the water park?

_____

4. Why did it take the Bouncing Beaver family so long to get to the water park?

_____

5. Where did the Bouncing Beaver family stay on their vacation?

_____

6. Do you think the Bouncing Beaver family would recommend the park to other beavers? Why or why not?

_____

Platypus

What a strange creature! The platypus has webbed feet like a duck. And it lays eggs like a duck! And oh, that nose! The nose of the platypus looks like the bill of a duck! But the platypus is a mammal, not a bird. It lives partly in water and partly on land.

So how do scientists know that this is a mammal and not a bird? An animal is classified as a mammal when its body is covered in fur. The platypus is furry. A mammal also feeds milk to its young. The platypus does this, too. Birds have feathers and wings, so the platypus is safely out of that group.

Where might you run into one of these interesting animals? The platypus lives along the eastern coast of Australia in small rivers and streams. It is mostly active at night, or on cloudy days. The Australians are proud that the platypus makes their country its home. The animal is a national mascot at some events, and it even appears on the back of one of their coins.

The nose, or snout, of a platypus does not work like the bill of a duck. It does not open and close like a mouth. The snout works like a regular nose. The platypus has a mouth underneath the snout.

At one time, people hunted this animal for its fur. Now laws protect the animal. Everyone wants to see this amazing creature on Earth for a long time to come.

Read each question. Circle the correct answer.

1. What kind of animal is a platypus?

a. bird

b. mammal

c. fish

d. reptile

2. What kind of feet does the platypus have?

a. claws

b. flippers

c. webbed feet

d. tails

3. Where does the platypus live?

a. on land only

b. in water only

c. partly in water and partly on land

d. none of the above

4. In what country can you find the platypus?

a. the United States

b. Japan

c. Australia

d. Greenland

5. What makes the platypus like a bird?

a. Its nose looks like a duck's bill.

b. Its tail looks like a duck's tail.

c. It quacks like a duck.

d. It has wings.

6. Why did people used to hunt the platypus?

a. for its bones

b. for its meat

c. for its beak

d. for its fur

Garage Sale

Mike and his dad were running a garage sale. It took them all week to get ready for it. First, they decided what they wanted to sell and they put it neatly in the garage. Mike had a lot of old toys and clothes he wanted to get rid of. His dad said he could keep any money he made from the items he sold.

Mike's dad found a lot of things to get rid of. He had an old desk, four chairs, an old lawn mower, two extra bowling balls, old golf clubs, as well as many boxes of household items. Mike found everything he wanted to sell pretty quickly but all week his dad kept finding more and more stuff. The pile in the garage kept getting bigger and bigger with things to sell.

The last thing Mike did for his dad before the sale was make signs. They had to let people know where and when the sale was going to be. He used thick black markers and some old cardboard boxes to make the signs. When he was done he had seven signs in all. The day before the sale they went out together to staple the signs to telephone poles.

GARAGE SALE!

As the sale started, they opened the garage door. They spread some things out onto the driveway for people to see. Mike and his dad were busy right away. People kept pulling up to the house all day and buying the things Mike's dad had collected. Once in a while Mike sold an item or two from his pile.

On the second day they were just as busy. Someone bought a whole box of Mike's old toys. When they counted the money they had made, they realized the sale brought in almost $200! What did they do with it? They bought more stuff!

Number the events in the correct order according to the story.

_____ They opened the garage door and spread items out.

_____ They added more to the pile.

_____ They bought more stuff.

_____ They stapled the signs to telephone poles.

_____ Mike and his dad put piles of things in the garage.

_____ They made signs.

_____ They counted almost $200 from the sale.

A Good Forest Fire?

We have always been warned about the dangers of forest fires. They cause damage to a forest. They kill many plants and animals in an ecosystem, which is a community of living things and their environment. But have you ever heard of a forest fire that can be good for a forest? Some are started on purpose to actually help the ecosystem.

In fact, fires are a natural part of any ecosystem. Without fires, the oldest and largest trees would block sunlight from reaching the forest floor. Fires can get rid of some of this old growth. When the old tree dies, its nutrients are added to the soil. New trees can grow strong and healthy in their place.

Some trees even need fires to grow. The pine trees found in some forests hold their seeds inside cones. Heat from a fire allows the cones to open up. Then the seeds fall to the ground and have a chance to grow.

Ecologists, who know about nature's needs, start some of these fires, called controlled burns. A fire is started and kept under control. This way, the fire does not spread out of the area or cover too much of the forest. Fires can be dangerous for animals. Even when animals survive forest fires, they can starve because their food supplies have been damaged in the fire. Small, controlled fires mean that animals will not have to travel too far to find food. These fires also make it easier for animals to travel to a new home after a fire. After some time, small plants begin to grow. Animals return shortly after the plants return, and again form an ecosystem.

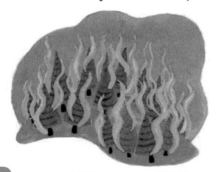

So the next time you hear about a forest fire, think about the good as well as the bad. It may take a new ecosystem a while to return, but it will likely come back stronger and healthier than ever.

Read each question. Circle the correct answer.

1. What is the meaning of an *ecosystem*?

   a. a place where plants and animals live

   b. a place where fires are made

   c. a place where scientists work

   d. a place where students go to school

2. What is an *ecologist*?

   a. a person who studies animals

   b. a person who studies nature

   c. a person who studies water

   d. a person who studies danger

3. What is the meaning of a *controlled burn*?

   a. a fire that does not burn as hot as other fires

   b. a fire that does not burn in forests

   c. a fire that is kept under control so that it does not get too big

   d. a burn that someone gets from a forest fire

4. How can a controlled burn be used?

   a. to help new growth survive in a forest

   b. to help animals find a new home

   c. to control where plants grow

   d. to make a fire spread over a large area

5. What is the first to return after a forest fire?

   a. deer

   b. birds

   c. small plants

   d. full-grown trees

6. How can a fire help some pinecones?

   a. They grow faster in fire.

   b. They would grow too big without fire.

   c. They can be found more easily by animals.

   d. The cones open up from heat and drop seeds.

The Dive

I climb the high ladder to the platform above. I take a deep breath. The pool water looks like a sparkling diamond from up here. The sun is hitting the water at just the right angle. Soon I'll break the stillness of that water like a torpedo.

I reach the top step and hop to the platform with an excited spring in my step. I shake my arms and hands to loosen up. I jump lightly in place and then come to a complete stop.

Now I am ready for my dive. It's all my mind can think about. I block out everything else around me.

I walk to the end of the platform. It springs back with each step I take. I curl my toes around the edge of the board.

I raise my hand to the judge. Now it is time. As I soar through the air, my legs stay together as if they are tied. My toes are pointed. My arms reach down to touch my toes. Then my legs flip out behind me. I come to a stiff and straight position as my body falls into the water below. I am as straight as an arrow and my fingertips reach the cool water first.

Splash! I am in. The dive is done. It felt right. I hold my breath. My arms and legs move together and in no time I am back up to the top of the water. I can hear the sound of the applause through my water-filled ears. In a moment the sounds are clear. I did it!

Number the events in the correct order according to the story.

_____ I soar through the air with my legs together.

_____ I block out everything from my mind.

_____ I hear applause through my water-filled ears.

_____ I climb the ladder.

_____ I raise my hand to the judge.

_____ I shake my arms and hands to loosen up.

_____ I curl my toes around the edge of the board.

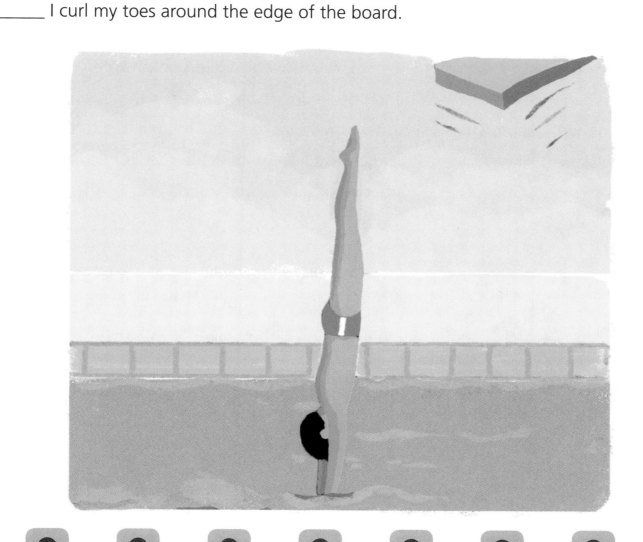

The Greatest Magician on Earth

Who was the greatest magician who ever lived? He escaped from a locked, water-filled milk container. He escaped from a straightjacket while hanging from the side of a building—upside down! It was Harry Houdini. Born in 1874 in Hungary, Houdini, whose real name was Ehrich Weiss, later moved to the United States with his family. It was there that he began to dream of becoming a magician. He began his career with card tricks and changed his name to Harry Houdini. He took the name to honor another magician who had the last name of Houdin.

Then Houdini found that people loved to watch magic escape tricks. So he turned his act to this kind of magic. His magic act quickly became famous. He escaped from handcuffs, chains, ropes, and locks. Sometimes he escaped all four together.

In Houdini's most famous trick, he had to hold his breath underwater for more than three minutes. First, he was hung upside down in a container that was overflowing with water. Then the container was locked and Houdini had to escape from it unharmed. His magic acts were always filled with danger and difficult escapes. Other magicians would not dare to try them because of this.

Houdini's act was famous at a time before television. He could not be seen by millions of people on a TV show. He performed in front of live audiences in packed theaters or concert halls. His tricks had to be done over and over again at each show. But people loved to watch him, no matter what he did. Houdini, the world's greatest magician, died on Halloween in 1926.

Read each question. Circle the correct answer.

1. Which of these is an *opinion* from the reading?

   a. Houdini had to hold his breath underwater for more than three minutes.

   b. Ehrich Weiss was born in 1874 in Hungary.

   c. Houdini was the greatest, most famous magician in the world.

   d. Houdini escaped from a locked, water-filled milk container.

2. Which of these is a *fact* from the reading?

   a. People love to watch magic escape tricks.

   b. Houdini was the greatest magician in the world.

   c. People loved to watch Houdini do magic.

   d. Houdini escaped from a straightjacket while hanging from a building.

3. What was the name of the magician that Houdini admired?

   a. Weiss

   b. Houdini

   c. Houdin

   d. Ehrich

4. According to the reading, which of the following did Houdini **not** escape from?

   a. handcuffs

   b. chains

   c. ropes

   d. vines

5. What did Houdini use in his first tricks?

   a. handcuffs

   b. straightjacket

   c. cards

   d. milk containers

6. What did other magicians think of Houdini's act?

   a. It was too easy for them.

   b. It was too dangerous for them.

   c. It was not interesting.

   d. It was too long.

The Skateboarder

Marcus was the best skater in his town. No one could make a skateboard move like he could. But last week Marcus wiped out on his board and broke his ankle. He was doing a trick in the park and the board slipped out from under him. His older brother rushed him to the hospital. The doctor patched him up in just a few minutes.

"Even the best skaters have to be careful," the doctor told him. He would not be able to skateboard for at least two months. Marcus was sure it would be the worst two months of his life. All of his friends went to the park without him. As he watched them he even thought his friend Josh was getting to be a better skater than he was.

As he sat on the park bench each day he read skateboard magazines. He learned about new tricks, famous skaters, and the history of skating. After about a week, Marcus didn't worry about what he was missing or what his friends were doing. He read old issues of the magazines. He especially enjoyed an article in one of the magazines called "From the Skaters." Young skaters just like him wrote the articles. They wrote about the experiences they had and what they want to learn.

Marcus decided to write about breaking his ankle. He carefully wrote his story and sent it to the magazine. He did not even care if the magazine printed his article. He liked the idea of writing about skateboarding so much he kept writing more stories and sending them to the magazine. Because of his accident, he had discovered a new hobby.

Read each question. Circle the correct answer.

1. Why couldn't Marcus skate with his friends?

a. He broke his ankle.

b. He got in trouble in school.

c. He lost his skateboard.

d. His skateboard was stolen.

2. Why did Marcus feel bad about not being able to skateboard?

a. He would lose the skateboard contest at school.

b. He would never be able to skate again.

c. He thought his friends were getting to be better skaters.

d. His friends did not like skating without him.

3. What did Marcus do when he couldn't skate?

a. He took pictures of the other skaters.

b. He read skateboard magazines.

c. He wrote articles for the school newspaper.

d. He taught other skaters new tricks.

4. What did Marcus decide to write about?

a. how to fix a broken ankle

b. what it was like to break an ankle while skating

c. how to get good grades in school

d. where to find old issues of magazines

5. What topics were **not** mentioned in the skating magazines?

a. new tricks

b. famous skaters

c. first aid

d. history of skating

6. What advice did the doctor give Marcus?

a. check your wheels

b. don't skate

c. jump higher

d. be careful

EPCOT

Have you ever been to EPCOT in Florida's Walt Disney World? EPCOT stands for the *Experimental Prototype Community of Tomorrow*. Walt Disney himself had the idea for the community. Back in the 1960s, Disney bought 28,000 acres of land in Orlando, Florida. He wanted this land to be used for his East Coast Disneyland. Disney wanted this new Disneyland to be filled with modern and fun ideas.

Disney wanted EPCOT to be a real place for people to live and work. EPCOT was to be the main attraction in the new Disneyland. Anyone visiting would have to enter and exit from EPCOT. American companies would be able to develop and test new technologies to be used within EPCOT. Visitors would be able to take tours of these companies.

Walt Disney worked on the project right up until his death on December 15, 1966. The company dropped the concept of EPCOT after Disney's death. His brother Roy continued to try and convince the board to build EPCOT as Walt had wanted it. The board instead decided to build the Magic Kingdom theme park. Roy Disney asked that the whole Orlando property be called Walt Disney World.

Of course, EPCOT eventually was built. But instead of an actual city, a theme park was built around Walt Disney's original concepts. Today, EPCOT is like a world's fair with the themes of science and technology. Many countries are represented in the park, giving guests a view of the various countries around the world.

Answer the questions below.

1. What does EPCOT stand for?

_____

2. Who thought of the idea for EPCOT?

_____

3. Why didn't the concept work out?

_____

4. What did Disney have in his mind for the idea of EPCOT?

_____

5. Who thought of the name Walt Disney World?

_____

6. What is today's EPCOT like?

_____

_____

_____

_____

_____

The Spider Essay

Steven Jones was the winner of this year's essay contest about a favorite animal. He chose to write about spiders. Most people don't think of spiders as their favorite animal, but Steven does. His essay was well written and had many interesting facts. People were surprised that an animal as spooky as a spider would be a contest winner.

All of Steven's friends cheered for him when he won. He went up on stage to get his award. He thanked his teachers and his parents for their help. He then took something out of a small box in his pocket. It was his pet tarantula named Specter. Some of the girls screamed when he took it out and let it crawl on his hand.

Then Steven was asked to read his essay aloud. That's when we all learned some facts about spiders. Did you know that spiders are not even insects? They are from another animal group called *arachnids*. Spiders have only two separate body parts. Insects have three. Spiders also have eight legs. Insects have six legs. Spiders make their own silk, which they use to help catch prey to eat. They catch flies and other insects in their webs. Then they wrap them up in their web and save them to eat later.

Everyone hates to see a spider in his or her house. But Steven's essay says that spiders eat other insects that might be a pest in a house or garden. Well, that's good to know!

Read each statement. Circle *fact* or *opinion*.

1. Steven Jones wrote an essay about spiders.　　　　fact　　　opinion

2. Most people don't like spiders.　　　　fact　　　opinion

3. People were surprised that the essay won.　　　　fact　　　opinion

4. Steven's friends cheered when he won.　　　　fact　　　opinion

5. Spiders are not insects.　　　　fact　　　opinion

6. Spiders have two body parts and
eight legs.

　　　fact　　　opinion

7. Everyone hates to see spiders.

　　　fact　　　opinion

8. It's good to know that spiders eat
other insects.

　　　fact　　　opinion

How to Fold an American Flag

The American flag is one of the most important symbols of our country. There is a special way to fold the American flag. If done correctly, the flag ends up in the shape of a triangle. The triangle shape honors the founders of our country by looking like the triangle-shaped hats that they used to wear.

To fold the flag, work with a partner. Hold the two short ends at the level of your waist. Have your partner hold the other two ends. Make sure the flag never touches the ground.

Then fold the bottom of the flag up to meet the top. Fold it again the same way. The flag should be in the shape of a long rectangle. The stars should be on the left side and the stripes on the right.

At this point the bottom end of the rectangle is folded and the top is open. Start with the striped end of the flag. Fold the corner into a triangle. The bottom corner should fold up to touch the top row. Now fold the triangle to the left and down. Then fold it to the left and up. Continue folding the flag in this triangle shape. One partner folds as the other holds the starred end and waits for the partner to get closer. Remember, the flag should never touch the ground. Continue folding so that your triangle gets thicker. Soon you will be left with a triangle with a square next to it.

The top, outside corner of the square should be folded down to make another triangle. It will look like one large triangle. But the thin side gets tucked into the larger side. The folds will stay in place until it is time to use it again. Then it gets unraveled with each step going in the opposite direction.

Read each statement. Write *true* or *false*.

1. The American flag should be folded into the shape of a square. _____

2. The American flag should never touch the floor. _____

3. It takes three people to fold the flag. _____

4. The flag should be folded into the shape of a rectangle twice. _____

5. The flag's stars should be on the right side. _____

6. The last step of folding the flag is tucking in the end. _____

7. The flag gets unraveled in the same way but in the opposite direction.

_____

8. It does not make a difference how the flag is folded. _____

Eiffel Tower

What would you hope to see if you took a trip to Paris? Most people put the Eiffel Tower at the top of their list. The Eiffel Tower has become the most famous symbol of this French city.

The tower was built for the International Exhibition of Paris of 1889. It was built to honor the 100-year anniversary of the French Revolution. The design was part of a contest. The design of Gustave Eiffel received every vote. However, that did not mean that everyone wanted the tower to be built. Some people thought the modern tower would look ugly in the middle of the old and beautiful city. Today, people around the world could not imagine the city without it.

The tower is over 1,000 feet tall and weighs over 7,000 tons. It's about the height of an 80-story building. For many years it was the tallest structure in the world. It took 300 steel workers two years to build the tower. They used 18,038 iron pieces held together by over 2 million rivets, which are metal pins. The very top of the tower can sway if the wind is very strong. The antenna at the top of the tower really works. It broadcasts French television and radio.

More than 200 million people have visited the tower since it was built. About 6 million people visit the tower each year. They don't have to climb the 1,665 steps to the top of the tower. Today people can take a set of elevators up through its three viewing platforms.

Answer the questions below.

1. When was the Eiffel Tower built?

_____

2. How tall is the Eiffel Tower?

_____

3. How much does the tower weigh?

_____

4. How many steel workers built the tower?

_____

5. How many steps does the tower have?

_____

6. How many iron pieces and rivets were needed to build the tower?

_____

7. What does the antenna do?

_____

8. How many people have visited the tower since it was built?

_____

The Olympics

One of the longest standing traditions of all time is the Olympics. There are written records of Olympic Games as far back as 776 B.C.E. At that Olympics there was just one event. It was a run of about 210 yards, which was won by a naked runner named Coroebus! It is believed that the Olympics were held many years before that date, but there is no written record of those games.

The first modern Olympics event was held in 1859 in Athens, Greece. The IOC, or the International Olympic Committee, was started in 1894. In 1896 the IOC had the first Summer Olympic Games. Athletes from all over the world participated.

As of 2006, the Summer Olympics include 28 sports and the Winter Olympics include 7 sports. Athletes train for years to compete in the Olympics. Only the very best athletes from each country can compete.

Before 1992, Olympic fans had to wait four years to see Olympic Games. Now fans have to wait only two years to see the games. The Winter Olympics and Summer Olympics alternate. For example, the Summer Olympics were held in 2000 and 2004, while the Winter Olympics occurred in 2002 and 2006.

Every Olympics is held in a different country. People love to visit from all around the world to see the city that is hosting the Olympics that year. The games can be seen on TV. Satellite images are broadcast into homes around the world. The games are

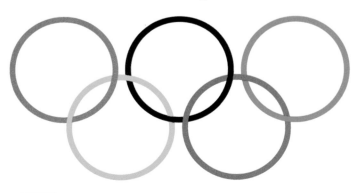

a great way to help countries put aside their problems. The stars of the Olympics are the athletes, not the country leaders. The Olympics even make many young people want to become athletes. Everyone loves watching the Olympic Games!

Read each statement. Write *fact* or *opinion*.

1. The Olympics are one of the longest standing traditions. _____

2. A runner name Coroebus won an Olympic running event. _____

3. The first modern Olympics were held in Athens, Greece. _____

4. People from all around the world love to visit the city that is hosting the Olympics that year. _____

5. Today, the Olympics are held every two years. _____

6. The games are a great way to help countries put aside their problems. _____

7. The Olympics make many young people want to become athletes. _____

8. Everyone loves watching the Olympic Games! _____

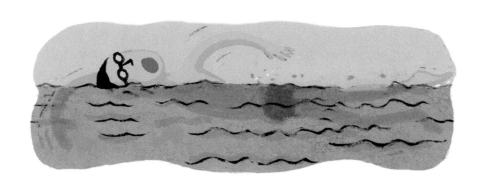

Solar Eclipse Day

Wednesday was a special day in school. The science teacher said there was going to be a solar eclipse. All classes after lunch were canceled and everyone went out into the schoolyard. The eclipse, explained the science teacher, happens when the moon passes between the earth and the sun. The sun's rays are blocked by the moon and less or none of its light reaches earth.

She warned us not to look directly at the sun. She said that even with the eclipse, the sun could damage our eyes. She handed out very thick and heavy dark glasses. They were so dark it was impossible to see anything with them. When we put them on, she said, we would be able to faintly see where the moon was passing in front of the sun. I looked up at the sky. The moon was blocking only part of the sun at first, but she told us that it takes a while for the full eclipse to happen. We were very lucky that it was not cloudy. If it was, we would not have been able to see the eclipse, and they only happen once every year. Suddenly the sky went completely dark. It looked as if it was nighttime for a few seconds.

Our teacher told us that there are four different kinds of eclipses: the total eclipse, which is when the sun is completely covered by the moon; the annular eclipse, which is when the sun and the moon are in line and it looks like there is a golden ring around the moon; the hybrid eclipse, when some parts of the earth see the eclipse as a total one and other parts of the earth see it as an annular eclipse. The fourth type of eclipse is the partial eclipse, which is when the sun and the moon are not in line and the moon only covers a part of the sun. The eclipse we saw was an annular eclipse. The teacher had a special digital camera she took pictures with. After a while we all went into the auditorium to look at the pictures on a big screen. The pictures were later hung up in the school hall for everyone to see.

Read each statement. Write *true* or *false*.

1. The students went outside to watch a lunar eclipse. _____

2. The teacher let them look at the eclipse through dark glasses. _____

3. The sun cannot damage the eyes during an eclipse. _____

4. The teacher took pictures of the eclipse with a digital camera. _____

5. The eclipse can be seen best on a cloudy day. _____

6. An eclipse happens when the moon passes between earth and the sun.

_____

7. More of the sun's rays reach earth during an eclipse. _____

8. Eclipses happen once a month. _____

Sacagawea

Today, we can take one of thousands of roads to get to the western United States. We can even take a plane there from anywhere in the world. But in the early 1800s, Native Americans were the only ones who knew the area as home. The famous Lewis and Clark expedition brought the first European explorers to the far western United States. A woman named Sacagawea helped the explorers find their way. She was from the Shoshone tribe in Idaho. She traveled on the trip with her husband, Toussaint Charbonneau.

The expedition was thousands of miles long. It started in St. Louis, Missouri, in 1804. When the travelers reached the head of the Missouri River, they needed someone to translate the Shoshone language. Sacagawea knew the language well and was willing to help. She was pregnant with her first child at the time, and Lewis assisted in the birth of her baby boy. The baby was named Jean Baptiste Charbonneau, but the expeditioners called him Little Pomp.

The Lewis and Clark expedition finally reached the Pacific coast in 1805. On their way back home they came upon the Rocky Mountains. Sacagawea offered some good advice. She said they should travel along the Yellowstone River basin. This route later became the way railroad lines crossed through the huge mountain range.

Today, Sacagawea is honored on a United States dollar coin. The image shows her carrying her son on her back. Sacagawea and her husband settled in St. Louis, Missouri, soon after the expedition. She gave birth to a baby girl sometime after 1810. Little is known about her later life. It is believed that she died in 1812 at the age of 25.

Read each statement. Write *true* or *false*.

1. Sacagawea was a woman from the Shoshone tribe. _____

2. Lewis and Clark hired Sacagawea to find the Pacific Ocean for them.

_____

3. Sacagawea traveled on the Lewis and Clark expedition with her husband.

_____

4. Sacagawea started the trip in 1804 with a newborn baby. _____

5. Sacagawea translated for the group. _____

6. Sacagawea's image is on a U.S. quarter. _____

7. Sacagawea told the group to walk along the Rocky Mountains.

_____

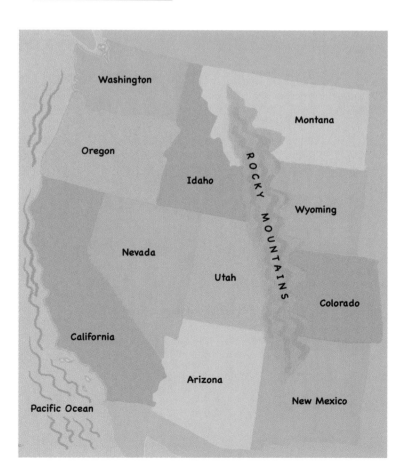

8. Sacagawea and her husband settled in St. Louis, Missouri.

_____

The Lost Keys

Jack Springer could not find his house keys. Now he was locked out of his own house. Jack often misplaced or lost things. Recently, he forgot his tuba on the school bus. A week before that he had lost his lunch. Earlier in the school year he even forgot that he had a day off and went to the school when it was closed. Now he had lost his keys. *Where could they be?* he thought.

He tried to remember when he had them last. He knew he took them to school that morning. His mother had handed them to him as he left the house. He also remembered having them when he paid for pizza on the lunch line. *Perhaps I lost them in the lunchroom*, he thought. Then he remembered gym class. He changed into his gym uniform and remembered taking them out and putting them in his gym locker.

"Ah-ha," he said aloud. "They are still in my locker."

Lucky for Jack, school was not too far. He grabbed his bike from the yard and pedaled fast, back to the school. There were still a few teachers there as well as the janitor. He explained what had happened and the janitor let him go back to his locker. He quickly turned the combination dial and opened the door. There were his keys, right where he had left them on the top shelf.

He biked home and let himself into the house with the keys. Later he told his parents what had happened. They were happy Jack had found his keys on his own. Jack was happy he had found them, too.

Match each word to its definition. Write the letter on the line.

1. _____ recently

a. clothes worn for a special purpose

2. _____ misplaced

b. moved by using pedals, such as on a bike

3. _____ uniform

c. happening not long ago

4. _____ janitor

d. forgot where it was placed

5. _____ pedaled

e. person who cleans or maintains a place

Answer the questions below.

6. Where had Jack left his keys?

_____

7. What does the phrase *on his own* in the last paragraph mean?

_____

8. Have you ever lost something important? Did you find it?

_____

_____

Killer Bees

You may have heard people say that a bee will leave you alone if you leave it alone. Well, that's almost always the case. There is a special kind of bee that will attack people without being bothered first. It is called an *Africanized honeybee*, or killer bee. These bees do not have a sting that is more dangerous than other bees, but they can be deadly because they attack in large groups, called swarms.

A person attacked by killer bees can become very sick, or even die. The bees can give a person hundreds of stings within a few minutes. They especially attack a person's head and face.

Where did such deadly bees come from? Scientists bred them in the 1950s. Scientists were trying to find a bee that could make honey better in warm climates such as South America. Some of the bees escaped and bred with local bees. Over the years, the bees spread to other areas in South America. Soon there were thousands of them.

The bees attack to protect their living areas. They do not usually attack people or animals unless they come into their area. But people and animals do not know that they are entering the bees' home. The bees can sense people by feeling vibrations of things such as cars. That's when they know to attack.

In recent years, the bees have been found in some of the southern states of the United States. The bees have been spotted in Texas, New Mexico, Arizona, Nevada, and California. They are only a little bit smaller than other honeybees, so it takes an expert to tell them apart. Your chances of being attacked by killer bees are slim. But be careful out there anyway!

Read each statement. Write *true* or *false*.

1. Killer bees will only attack when people hurt them. _____

2. A killer bee is also called an Africanized honeybee. _____

3. Killer bees have attacked people for hundreds of years. _____

4. Scientists bred killer bees. _____

5. Killer bees cannot live in warm climates. _____

6. Killer bees do not attack in swarms. _____

7. Killer bees sense vibrations to tell when people are near. _____

8. Killer bees do not live in the United States. _____

Leo the Cat

Mr. Bentley could not believe it when he heard his cat, Leo, talking. Leo really speaks English! He moves his mouth and tongue and real words come out of it! Mr. Bentley walked up to Leo in shock.

"Leo, you are a magic cat!" he cried.

"No, Mr. Bentley, I am not magic," Leo said. "All cats can talk. We just have to listen to people to learn the language. I listened to you and your friends talk for years. Now I am ready to practice what I have learned."

Mr. Bentley sat down on the couch in hopes that he would not faint. "You learned to talk from me?" he asked. "I have to tell people about this. I have to enter you in a show or a contest of some kind. Maybe we can win some money. I have never heard of a talking cat. People will be amazed."

Leo put his paw in the air. "No way," he said. "That will never happen. There's a reason nobody has heard of this. Cats have kept this secret for centuries. I am not going to be the kitty that spilled the beans," he said.

Mr. Bentley insisted. "Leo, this is a big deal. We could be famous!"

"No!" Leo put his whiskers and tail in the air and then hissed. "If you do not listen to me, then I cannot trust you to keep my secret."

Mr. Bentley was too greedy to keep Leo's secret. He told his friends what Leo did. They all sat around one night trying to get Leo to talk. Leo knew Mr. Bentley could not be trusted.

"Why won't he talk?" asked Mr. Bentley's friend, Sam.

Leo put his secret back in hiding. He never spoke again.

Read each statement. Write *true* or *false*.

1. Mr. Bentley is amazed that Leo can talk. _____

2. Leo learned to talk from watching television. _____

3. Leo is the only cat that can talk. _____

4. Mr. Bentley wants to enter Leo in a contest. _____

5. Leo is excited that he will become famous. _____

6. Leo asks that Mr. Bentley not tell
anyone his secret. _____

7. Mr. Bentley ruins Leo's secret.
_____

8. Leo becomes the first famous
talking cat. _____

What's Going on Hair?

Has anyone ever told you that you have nice hair? Did you ever wonder what hair is? It's really a kind of dead skin. All mammals have hair covering their bodies. People have tiny hairs covering most of their bodies. We do not have hair on our lips, eyelids, palms of the hands, and soles of the feet. But look at your skin carefully. You should be able to see tiny pores, or holes, where small pieces of skin grow. The hair on your head is, of course, the thickest and easiest to see. The hair is made of keratin, which is a kind of protein.

Hair does not grow back after it has been damaged. If you get a cut where there is hair, the skin will grow back and repair itself. But the hair will not grow back. You might have a scar where you were once hurt, but no hair will grow on the scar.

The average person loses about 100 hairs from their head a day. That's fine since there are about 100,000 follicles, or places for the hair to grow from your head.

An adult with very long hair has probably had that hair for a very long time. It takes about seven years to grow hair down to your waist. Hair grows faster in the summer. It slows down at night.

Answer the questions below.

1. What is hair made of?

_____

2. Where do people not have hair growing?

_____

3. What is keratin?

_____

4. What might happen to your hair if you were hurt and got a scar on your skin?

_____

5. Who has the oldest hair, a person with long or short hair? Why?

_____

6. Where does hair grow from?

_____

7. Is it normal to lose 90 hairs in one day? Why or why not?

_____

8. When does hair grow faster?

_____

John Henry

John Henry worked day after day as a steel driver for the Chesapeake and Ohio Railroad. One by one he hammered in those steel posts that laid the railroad track. No one could lay more tracks in a day than John Henry.

One day the railroad crew came across a giant mountain in front of them. Big Bend Mountain was a mile and a quarter thick. Instead of going all the way around the giant mountain, the crews had to dig their way right through the mountain to the other side. The crews could not even think about doing this giant task without the help of John Henry. He lay up to 12 feet of track in one day. It was double what any other worker could do.

Then one day the crews came to work and saw a new machine at the camp. There before them was a machine that could do the work of ten men. It was powered by steam and could drill into the mountain day and night without stopping.

The men did not want a machine to take their places. The only man who could challenge the machine was our hero, John Henry. The man and the machine went against each other. The crew stood by and cheered for our hero. By the end of the race, John Henry had drilled 14 feet of rock and the machine had only drilled 9 feet. The crowds cheered. Man had beaten machine. Or had he? John Henry collapsed at the end of the race and never woke up again. Today, travelers on the railroad can still see the face of John Henry in the rock at Big Bend Mountain.

Read each statement. Write *true* or *false*.

1. John Henry was a railroad conductor. _____

2. Workers had to dig through the middle of Big Bend Mountain. _____

3. John Henry could lay 100 feet of track in one day. _____

4. A machine at the camp could do the work of 10 men. _____

5. John Henry challenged the machine to lay railroad track. _____

6. John Henry drilled 9 feet of track and the machine drilled 14 feet. _____

7. The new machine was powered by steam. _____

8. John Henry collapsed for an hour after winning the race. _____

The Human Baby

Humans are mammals. Most mammals are born able to do many things. Deer can walk within a few minutes of being born. They have to be able to run away if danger is near. Human babies are born helpless. They need the care of adults to live.

In the first month of life, babies cannot smile or sit up. They cannot even hold up their own heads without some help from grown-ups. But even at this young age, babies are different from each other. Some sleep more than others. Some cry more than others. Some are more alert than others.

In the next few months, babies grow a lot. They learn to roll over, support their heads, and even sit up while being held. All of these things help a baby get ready to move, crawl, and sit on his or her own.

Babies also have to learn to use their hands. It takes months for them to learn to reach for objects. At around six months old many babies can move an object from one hand to another.

Babbling is how a human baby learns to speak. Babies all seem to make similar sounds. They try to imitate the sounds they hear from adults. It will take about nine months before a baby can say real words on his or her own.

Somewhere around a baby's first birthday he or she may stand or walk with help. Soon the baby will be running around on his or her own!

The first year of a baby's life is a time of growing and learning. A one-year-old baby may sleep about 15 hours a day, including nap-time. Growing sure takes a lot of work!

Number the baby stages in the correct order according to the reading.

_____ walk with no help

_____ roll over, support head

_____ stand and walk with help

_____ reach for objects

_____ say a word

_____ cannot smile or sit up

_____ move objects from hand to hand

The Fox and the Crow

Once there was a sly and clever fox. One day, the fox came upon a crow sitting in a tree. The crow held a large piece of cheese in its beak.

Now the fox knew that the crow would not simply give him the cheese just because he asked for it. He knew that he had to think of a sly way to get the cheese from the crow.

The fox thought and thought. Finally, he had an idea. He sat at the bottom of the tree and looked up at the crow thoughtfully.

"My, how beautiful you are," said the fox to the crow. "I have seen many birds in my time, but you are the most beautiful of all." The crow smiled but did not say a word.

"I'll bet your singing voice is as beautiful as you are," he said. "I have heard many crows sing but they do not have voices to match even a tiny bit of your good looks." The crow smiled again, but the cheese sat firmly in her beak.

"If you sing for me I would be so happy," the fox said. "I am sure your voice would fill these woods with joy."

The crow was so flattered that she began to sing a song for him. "Caw, caw, caw," began her song.

When the crow opened her mouth to sing, the cheese fell from her beak and through the branches of the tree. The sly fox caught the cheese in his mouth and ran away as quickly as he could.

"Your voice was not as beautiful as I had thought. In fact, you are not so cute, either. And not too smart for losing your meal!"

Answer the questions below.

1. Which animal has a piece of cheese in its mouth?

_____

2. What does the word _sly_ from paragraph 1 mean?

_____

3. Why does the fox tell the crow that she is beautiful?

_____

4. Does the fox really want to hear the crow sing? Why or why not?

_____

5. Why did the crow decide to start singing?

_____

6. What does the word _flattered_ from paragraph 7 mean?

_____

7. What happened as a result of the crow's singing?

_____

8. Why does the fox say that the crow is not smart?

_____

Pompeii

The city of Pompeii is a place frozen in time. This ancient city is near Naples, Italy. The city sits near the mighty volcano Mount Vesuvius. The mountain is 30 miles around and more than 4,000 feet tall. Mount Vesuvius had erupted many times throughout history. But the deadliest eruption happened during a two-day period in 79 A.D.

Vesuvius let out so much ash and other materials that it buried the town of Pompeii under 18 feet. Roofs collapsed from the weight of the ash. The eruption lasted for 19 hours. The ash rose from the volcano 20 miles into the air. The city of Pompeii, along with three other towns, was lost under the ash for almost 1,700 years.

Finally, in 1748, workers digging a canal uncovered this important city. What they found amazed the world. The city was left unchanged since that day in 79 A.D. The ash and mud from the volcano dried around animals, people, and objects. Over thousands of years this undisturbed area hardened to become rock. The 2,000 people who had died so suddenly were captured in time. They were frozen in the same positions in which they died. Some were clutching each other. Others were shielding themselves from the eruption.

Artwork, artifacts, tools, and everyday objects were found preserved in rock. It took years for the town to be uncovered. Scientists learned how people died as well as how they lived.

Today Pompeii is a popular place for tourists in Italy. People have again built around the area of Mount Vesuvius. People have even built homes halfway up the mountain. They can enjoy the beauty of the mountain. But can they escape the danger of another eruption?

Match each word to its definition. Write the letter on the line.

1. _____ ancient

a. materials that come out of a volcano

2. _____ artifacts

b. the act of a volcano becoming active

3. _____ ash

c. a mountain through which gases, rock, and materials can erupt

4. _____ collapsed

d. kept in an unchanged condition

5. _____ eruption

e. people who visit an area

6. _____ preserved

f. fallen

7. _____ tourists

g. objects made by humans

8. _____ volcano

h. very old

Surf's Up

Gerry was excited. Gerry was frightened. Gerry did not know what to feel anymore. He was about to go surfing for the first time.

He had watched his brother Keith surf on family vacations. It looked like so much fun to him. He would love to ride a wave like his brother did. But he knew it would take practice. He was afraid of falling. And his mom's warnings about getting hurt sure didn't help him to feel better about it.

But the day had come. He wore his brother's old wetsuit. He held his brother's old surfboard out in front of his body.

"You'll be fine, Gerry," said Keith. "Just follow my lead. And do not try to stand up this first time. It will take a while before you can stand."

"Okay," said Gerry. The two brothers walked out into the water. Then they lay down on the boards to swim out against the waves.

"Be careful," yelled Mom from the shore.

Finally they reached a deep and calm part of the water. "See that wave rolling in?" asked Keith. "Just as it starts to rock you a little, make your body hop on the board at the same time. Then we'll just ride it in like that. Mom will like it if we take it easy on the first wave." Gerry thought that Keith could see he was nervous, but he didn't care.

"Okay," said Gerry. "We'll take it easy on this one."

"Now!" yelled Keith, as the wave rolled in. They both jumped up so they were lying on the boards. A small smile popped up on Gerry's face. His smile got wider as the wave carried him to shore.

He looked up to see his mom smiling at him. "Pretty cool," she said.

Gerry felt great. He was ready to try again.

Number the events in the correct order according to the story.

_____ Keith warns Gerry not to stand up.

_____ Gerry feels great and wants to try again.

_____ The boys jump up on their boards to ride the wave to shore.

_____ Mom yells that the boys should be careful.

_____ Gerry feels nervous.

_____ Gerry sees a wave coming.

_____ Keith and Gerry reach a deep part of the water.

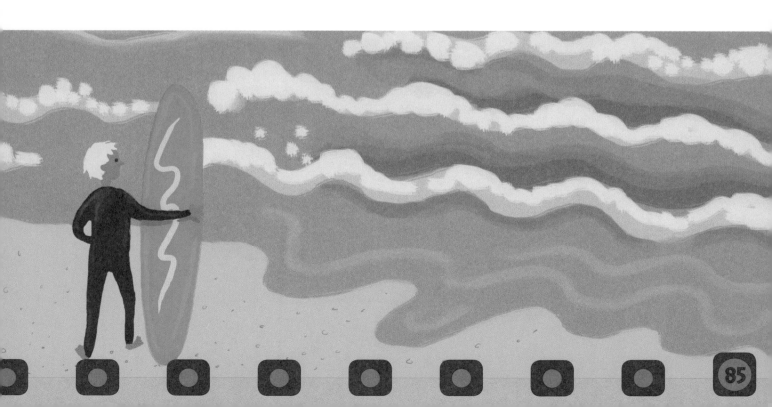

How to Make Great Cookies

1 cup flour

$\frac{1}{2}$ teaspoon baking soda

$\frac{1}{2}$ teaspoon salt

1 stick softened butter

$\frac{3}{4}$ cup sugar

$\frac{1}{2}$ teaspoon vanilla extract

1 egg

1 cup chocolate chips

Have an adult help you to preheat the oven to 375 degrees. Then mix the first three ingredients on the list in a small bowl. Using a hand mixer, mix together the butter, sugar, and vanilla. Then slowly beat in the egg and then the flour mixture. Mix it until it looks like dough. Stir in the chocolate chips by hand until they are mixed into the dough well. Roll small pieces of the dough into balls. Place them on an ungreased cookie sheet. Make sure all of the balls are the same size. This will help them all cook evenly. Put the cookies into the oven for about 10 minutes. Take them out of the oven when they are golden brown. After they have cooled for a few minutes, use a spatula to take the cookies off the sheet. Place them on a wire rack until they cool all the way. Then eat them with a glass of milk. Delicious!

Read each statement. Write *true* or *false*.

1. The recipe calls for a cup of butter. _____

2. The same amount of flour and chocolate chips are used. _____

3. The same amount of salt and sugar are used. _____

4. The cookie sheet should be greased before the cookies are placed on it.

_____

5. The sugar, butter, and vanilla should be mixed with a fork. _____

6. The dough should be rolled into balls. _____

7. The cookies are done when they are golden brown. _____

8. Take the cookies off the baking sheet when they have cooled a few minutes.

_____

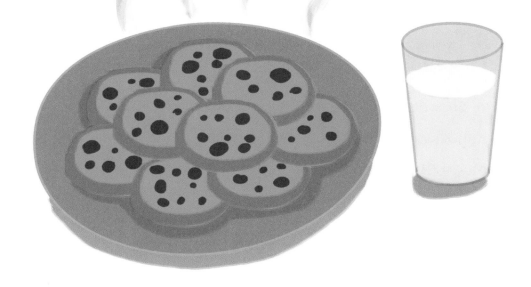

Margot's Sculpture

Margot read her homework assignment for the third time. She had to make a piece of art out of used or thrown-away items. How was she going to do this?

She asked Dad what he thought of such a strange homework assignment.

"Well, that's a pretty good idea," he said. "A lot of people throw too much stuff away. Our landfills get crowded. Sometimes they become full. If we used more stuff over again we would cut down on garbage. It's called recycling. Making art out of garbage sounds like a really fun project."

Margot stared at him. *Really?* she thought. *Fun?* He showed her an art book from the bookshelf. There was a piece of art made of old bicycle tires. "If you throw out bike tires they will sit in the landfills forever. They do not break down like some other materials. So here's a good way to reuse something that we no longer need."

"I think I get it," Margot said. "Maybe I'll peek through the garbage can and see if I can make a sculpture or something." She carefully looked through the can. She found an empty milk carton, paper clips, and a sock with a hole in it. She took them out and cleaned them off. Then she looked around her bedroom for some things she did not need.

She worked in her room with the items for what seemed like hours. Then she brought her finished sculpture to Dad.

"Here it is!" she said proudly. "It's a sculpture of a dinosaur. He has a milk carton body, a sock tail, and paper clip spikes down his back. He's ready for an art museum!"

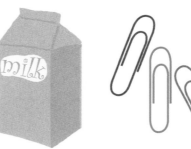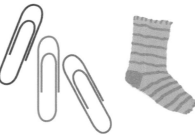

"And just a little while ago he was pieces of garbage!" said Dad.

Answer the questions below.

1. How did Margot feel about her assignment at the beginning of the story?

_____

2. Why did Margot ask her dad to help her with the assignment?

_____

3. What does the word *recycling* in paragraph 3 mean?

_____

4. Why is it a good idea to reuse things instead of throw them away?

_____

5. Where did Margot get the items to make her sculpture?

_____

6. What would happen to bike tires if they were thrown away?

_____

7. What did she use to make her dinosaur?

_____

8. How does Margot feel about her assignment by the end of the story?

_____

Getting Around Town

Just 100 years ago there were no fast planes, fast cars, or fast trains. Getting from place to place took a long time. People had to travel for days on wagons pulled by horses. And the roads the horses traveled on were not paved. They were bumpy dirt roads. That means in bad weather they became a muddy mess.

Cars were invented to make travel easier. But not many people could afford a car when they were first invented. Once cars were cheap enough for more people to buy, roads had to be built. Today, there are highways and roads connecting all parts of the United States. Cars can travel fast on highways. They need to stop less often than in the past.

Goods can travel much faster today than in the past. Today's freight trains go faster than trains 100 years ago. Today they can use electric power to go from station to station. In the past, coal was burned to make steam power. The engines were loud and made the air dirty. Today's trains run faster and cleaner than before. They can carry heavy loads of goods across the country easily.

Planes were invented in the early 1900s. They flew short distances and carried few people. Today giant planes carry hundreds of people at a time around the world.

We are lucky to live in a world where traveling is fast and easy. Transportation is always improving. What do you think traveling will be like in the future?

Complete the Venn diagram. Compare transportation today and in the past.
One is done for you.

Past   **Both**   **Present**

horse-drawn wagons

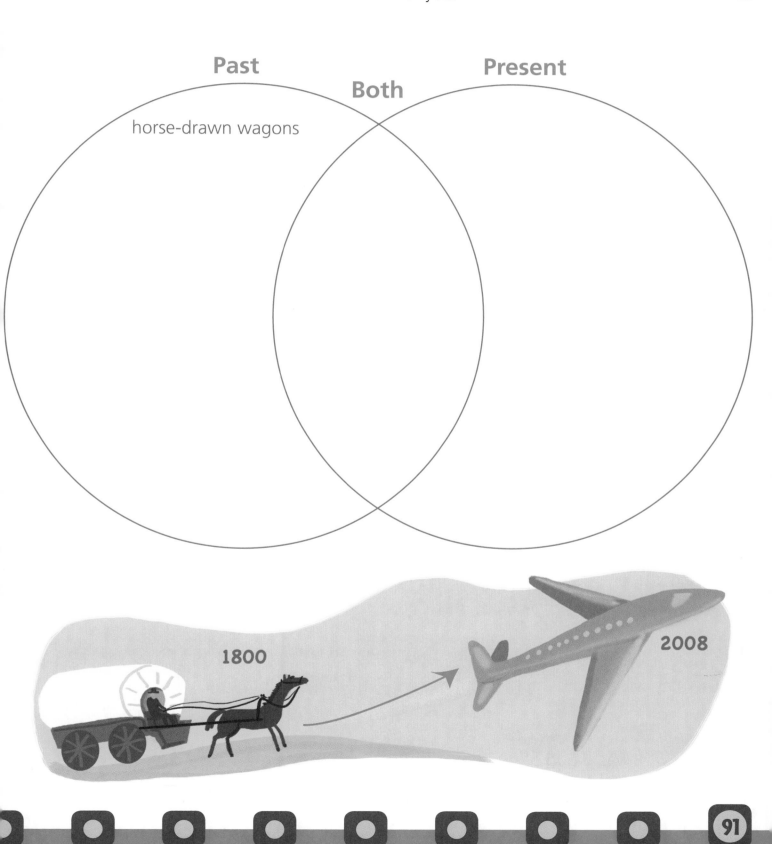

1800   2008

A Letter to the Police

Craig looked out the window of his apartment. Another car went screeching by in the street below. "Why do they have to go so fast?" he asked his mother.

"I don't know, but someone could really get hurt out there," said Mom. "I wonder if there's something we can do about it. I would hate for someone to get hurt and to think that we could have stopped it somehow."

"We can write a letter to the police to tell them that our road has become dangerous. There are too many fast drivers zooming past our apartment," said Craig.

"Good idea," said Mom. "You tell me what to write and I'll type it on my computer."

"Okay," said Craig. "Um, Dear Police…" He thought for a moment longer. "I live at 1238 Overlook Street. I hear cars screeching and zooming past our house at all hours of the day and night. These cars are driving at an unsafe speed. If they don't slow down I am sure they are going to hurt someone someday."

"Okay," said Mom. "Hold on. I've almost got it."

"I'm not done," said Craig. "There's more. Write this: I cannot tell their exact speed, but I know the cars are going too fast. The speed sign on the road says 35 miles per hour. I guess that these cars are going at least 50 miles per hour. Can you do something to help us? Sincerely, Craig Ryan."

Mom finished typing. "I think that is a good letter. Let's send it out today. I am sure they will do something about the problem. They might put a police officer on our street."

Craig was proud of his letter. He wondered how else he could help his community.

Answer the questions below.

1. What did Craig want to tell the police?

_____

2. How did they write the letter?

_____

3. What is Craig's address?

_____

4. How fast did Craig think the cars were going on his street?

_____

5. How might people get hurt on Craig's street?

_____

6. Why do you think Craig's mom thinks they might put police on the street?

_____

7. When are Craig and his mom going to send the letter?

_____

8. Craig wonders how else he can help his community. What are some ideas?

_____

Answer Key

Answers to some of the pages may vary.

Page 5
1. c
2. d
3. b
4. d
5. c
6. b

Page 7
1. a way to make something imaginary look real on film
2. makeup, fake blood, animal suits
3. to make it easier to film something
4. They program a model into the computer.
5. combine, mix together
6. They act in front of a screen. Computers add the special effects character later.

Page 9
1. proud
2. to enter it in a car show
3. He loves cars, and he wants to compare the cars to his own.
4. nervous
5. hot rods, muscle cars, custom-built cars, and family cars
6. less nervous about his car

Page 11
1. New York Knickerbockers
2. hitting him with the ball
3. 100
4. soldiers
5. 1871
6. more

Page 13
1. Emily's town has gotten more than 10 feet of snow.
2. to tell Grandma about the recent snowstorms
3. Grandma lives in Florida where it does not usually snow.
4. catch up, or be able to rest for a moment
5. to show Grandma snow from the big storm
6. Answers may vary.

Page 15
1. c
2. b
3. b
4. c
5. a
6. c

Page 17
1. Boy's face blows up like a balloon.
2. Games must stop and dogs are in danger.
3. Dogs may run into the busy street.
4. The dogs make a mess of the park.
5. to convince, or persuade, the mayor to make a rule that requires dogs to be on leashes in Lincoln Park
6. possible answers: fact: Lincoln Park is on Main Street; opinion: A new rule will help the park.

Page 19
1. Ozzie was turning twelve and should do more around the house.
2. He did not want to bother doing more work.
3. He thought about the comic books he would be able to buy with more money.
4. He had to ask his parents for more money when he wanted something.
5. on his first night of being twelve
6. First, he gathered garbage bags from around the house. He tied them up and put them in the can, which he rolled to the curb for pickup.

Page 21
1. They travel west.
2. Mules are used to plow fields.
3. Crops fail.
4. They decide they must move to California.
5. Many people move to California.
6. The mules will pull the family's wagon to California.

Page 23
1. a
2. c
3. d
4. a
5. c
6. b

Page 25
1. It makes your guests feel welcome.
2. watch a movie projected on the outside of the house
3. chips, cookies, popcorn, and drinks
4. They voted about what movie to watch. *The Wizard of Oz* won the vote.
5. big plastic bowls
6. glad that her preparations paid off

Page 27
4 Raffaelle Esposito made a special pizza for the queen.
3 Queen Margherita tasted a pizza for the first time.
5 American soldiers tasted pizza in Italy.
1 The Greeks enjoyed flat, baked breads.
6 Pizza became a popular food in the United States.
2 Pizza became a popular meal sold in Italy's streets.

Page 29
1. worried
2. helpful
3. carefree
4. scared
5. caring
6. happy

Page 31
1. They find an underground cave.
2. They find that they are from 15,000 or 13,000 B.C.E.
3. 1,200 people a day visit the cave.
4. The gas damages the paintings over time.
5. A copy of the cave is made for people to explore.
6. They learn about the lives of people who lived long ago.

Page 33
1. true
2. true
3. true
4. false
5. false
6. true

Page 35

Vitamin	How it helps the body	Found in
Vitamin A	eyesight, skin, teeth	carrots, tomatoes, sweet potatoes, pumpkins
Vitamin B	gives body energy	spinach, beef, chicken, tuna, eggs, milk, sunflower seeds, soymilk
Vitamin C	keeps from getting a cold	oranges, strawberries, mango, spinach, broccoli, snow peas
Vitamin D	good for bones	eggs, milk, fish
Vitamin E	keeps body's cells healthy	plant oils, avocados, whole grains
Folate	makes new cells in the body	green beans, broccoli, spinach, beans

Page 37
1. b
2. d
3. c
4. d
5. c
6. a

Page 39
1. The baby is a real cutie. But as far as I know, right now she is sleeping.
2. You and I are best friends forever. And in my opinion, you should check your e-mail every day to see if I've written.
3. In any case, I was just kidding about telling you to mind your own business. You are a great friend and always make me laugh out loud.
4. Oh my gosh, that was the funniest movie. We were all falling on the floor laughing. Way to go for choosing it for us.
5. Hold on a second, my mom is calling. I've got to go; it's time for dinner.
6. Sorry, this is the end of discussion. Hugs and kisses, and bye for now.

Page 41
1. the Log River Water Park
2. a beaver named Chuck
3. beavers
4. They had to walk many miles through forests and across roads.
5. beaver cabins
6. Yes; they had fun at the park and there is nothing else like it for beavers.

Page 43
1. b
2. c
3. c
4. c
5. a
6. d

Page 45
5 They opened the garage door and spread items out.
2 They added more to the pile.
7 They bought more stuff.
4 They stapled the signs to telephone poles.
1 Mike and his dad put piles of things in the garage.
3 They made signs.
6 They counted almost $200 from the sale.

Page 47
1. a
2. b
3. c
4. a
5. c
6. d

Page 49
6 I soar through the air with my legs together.
3 I block out everything from my mind.
7 I hear applause through my water-filled ears.
1 I climb the ladder.
5 I raise my hand to the judge.
2 I shake my arms and hands to loosen up.
4 I curl my toes around the edge of the board.

Page 51
1. c
2. d
3. c
4. d
5. c
6. b

Page 53
1. a
2. c
3. b
4. b
5. c
6. d

Page 55
1. Experimental Prototype Community of Tomorrow
2. Walt Disney
3. Disney died and the company wanted to build the Magic Kingdom theme park instead.
4. a real community for people to live and work and test new technologies
5. Walt Disney's brother, Roy Disney
6. a world's fair with a science and technology theme, and many countries from around the world are represented there

Page 57
1. fact
2. opinion
3. opinion
4. fact
5. fact
6. fact
7. opinion
8. opinion

Page 59
1. false
2. true
3. false
4. true
5. false
6. true
7. true
8. false

Page 61
1. 1889
2. over 1,000 feet
3. over 7,000 tons
4. 300
5. 1,665
6. 18,038 iron pieces, over 2 million rivets
7. broadcasts French television and radio
8. over 200 million

Page 63
1. fact
2. fact
3. fact
4. opinion
5. fact
6. opinion
7. opinion
8. opinion

Page 65
1. false
2. true
3. false
4. true
5. false
6. true
7. false
8. false

Page 67
1. true
2. true
3. true
4. false
5. true
6. false
7. false
8. true

Page 69
1. c
2. d
3. a
4. e
5. b
6. in his gym locker
7. without help from anyone else
8. Answers may vary.

Page 71
1. false
2. true
3. false
4. true
5. false
6. false
7. true
8. false

Page 73
1. true
2. false
3. false
4. true
5. false
6. true
7. true
8. false

Page 75
1. keratin, a kind of dead skin
2. lips, eyelids, palms of hands, soles of feet
3. a kind of protein
4. the hair would not grow back on that part of your skin
5. long hair; it takes a long time for hair to grow long
6. tiny holes called follicles
7. Yes. The average person loses about 100 hairs per day.
8. in the summer and during the day

Page 77
1. false
2. true
3. false
4. true
5. true
6. false
7. true
8. false

Page 79
7 walk with no help
2 roll over, support head
6 stand and walk with help
3 reach for objects
5 say a word
1 cannot smile or sit up
4 move objects from hand to hand

Page 81
1. the crow
2. smart, intelligent, clever
3. He wants to get the cheese away from her.
4. No. He wants her to open her mouth and drop the cheese.
5. She was flattered that the fox thought she had a nice voice.
6. to be complimented
7. She dropped the cheese from her mouth and the fox ran away with it.
8. Because she could be tricked into giving up her piece of cheese.

Page 83
1. h
2. g
3. a
4. f
5. b
6. d
7. e
8. c

Page 85
2 Keith warns Gerry not to stand up.
7 Gerry feels great and wants to try again.
6 The boys jump up on their boards to ride the wave to shore.
3 Mom yells that the boys should be careful.
1 Gerry feels nervous.
5 Gerry sees a wave coming.
4 Keith and Gerry reach a deep part of the water.

Page 87
1. false
2. true
3. false
4. false
5. false
6. true
7. true
8. true

Page 89
1. At the beginning she did not like it or understand it.
2. Margot did not understand the assignment at first so she needed some ideas.
3. using things over again
4. Reusing items helps to keep landfills from filling up too fast.
5. from the garbage
6. They would not break down like other items.
7. empty milk carton, paper clips, and a sock with a hole in it
8. At the end she thought it was fun.

Page 91
Past
horse-drawn wagons, dirt roads, early cars were expensive and slower, trains were loud and made air dirty, planes flew short distances with few people
Present
cars are faster and less expensive for people to buy, roads and highways connect the country, trains are faster and cleaner, planes fly long distances with a lot of people
Both
helped people and goods get from place to place

Page 93
1. Cars drive too fast on his street.
2. Craig told his mom what to type on the computer.
3. 1238 Overlook Street
4. about 50 miles per hour
5. They can get hit by a car.
6. She thinks the letter is good and that the police will want to help.
7. today or same day
8. Answers may vary.